J. S. BACH
SIX ENGLISH SUITES
BWV 806–811 FOR THE KEYBOARD

EDITED BY HANS BISCHOFF

AN ALFRED MASTERWORK EDITION

Copyright © 2015 by Alfred Music
All rights reserved. Printed in USA.
ISBN-10: 1-4706-2283-1
ISBN-13: 978-1-4706-2283-1

Cover art: Still Life with a Volume of Wither's *Emblemes* (1696)
By Edwaert Collier (Dutch, ca. 1642–1708)
Oil on canvas

No part of this book shall be reproduced, arranged, adapted, recorded, publicly performed, stored in a retrieval system, or transmitted by any means without written permission from the publisher. In order to comply with copyright laws, please apply for such written permission and/or license by contacting the publisher at alfred.com/permissions.

JOHANN SEBASTIAN BACH

Contents

About Hans Bischoff and This Edition 2

Foreword 3

Table of Embellishments 7

SIX ENGLISH SUITES

    Suite No. 1 in A Major, BWV 806 8

    Suite No. 2 in A Minor, BWV 807 28

    Suite No. 3 in G Minor, BWV 808 48

    Suite No. 4 in F Major, BWV 809 66

    Suite No. 5 in E Minor, BWV 810 84

    Suite No. 6 in D Minor, BWV 811 105

ABOUT HANS BISCHOFF AND THIS EDITION

Hans Bischoff (1852–1889) was a German concert pianist, chamber musician, and music educator. He studied piano with Theodor Kullak (1818–1882) and later taught piano performance and music theory at Kullak's school, Neue Akademie der Tonkunst, in Berlin. Bischoff became a well-regarded music editor, respected for his thorough research, attention to detail, and careful consideration of source materials. His critical editions for the Steingräber publishing house include seven volumes of the keyboard works by J. S. Bach and 11 volumes of the keyboard works by Robert Schumann, as well as editions of works by Clementi, Handel, Mozart, Schubert, and Weber.

Bischoff's footnotes and prefatory commentary have been preserved in this edition, as well as his editorial markings—suggested dynamics, metronome marks, fingering, articulations, and pedaling. Measure numbers and BWV numbers have been added. Square brackets have been used to indicate suspected missing elements from earlier Bischoff editions.

Six English Suites, BWV 806–811
Edited by Hans Bischoff

Foreword

Since I am issuing a new edition of the Bach Suites, may I first be permitted to express my gratitude to the libraries and individuals who have provided me with such a wealth of manuscript source-material, the extent of which has, in my opinion, never been available to any previous editor. It is a well-established fact that Bach had made many copies and recopies of his own works; the original form of the composition was frequently altered in these later copies. One can detect signs of the composer's indefatigable desire for improvement in almost all the movements of the French Suites. It is, therefore, not at all surprising to find two or more authentic documents contradicting each other. The instrinsic difficulty in editing lies in the necessity of establishing which of the various versions of a work, or portion of a work, represents Bach's ultimate intention, i.e., which version he would himself have chosen as the one best suited for publication. It is, therefore, exceedingly important to be familiar with the sequence in which various autographs of the same composition were written. Criticism of the text is made increasingly difficult by the fact that some of the corrections contained in a particular manuscript may be traced to an alien handwriting. One can readily perceive the importance of securing the most exhaustive collection of authoritative manuscripts for all the numerous works of Bach which did not appear in print during his own lifetime. Conjectural criticism, which cannot be avoided entirely in instances of uncertain tradition, must be based on the exhaustive study of the most thorough source-material. Previously published editions of the French Suites, some of which were doubtless edited with care—(the English Suites have not undergone as many transformations as the French Suites)—all share a common limitation in that they faithfully follow only the one particular document in the possession of the editor. I could even cast a most serious aspersion upon the Bach-Gesellschaft edition, particularly because it has won such monumental acclaim through the work of the highly deserving Dr. W. Rust and other musicological leaders—in that the editing of the Suites by an unnamed person is as ill-befitting as the editing of the Inventions by Mr. C. F. Becker.

We possess the following works of Bach written in suite form: the three well-known collections of the six French Suites, the six English Suites, the six Partitas, the French Partitas, a Suite in F major, the Suites in A minor, E-flat major, E minor, also a few fragments.

For historical and pedagogical reasons it is best to consider the French Suites first. I believe it is proper, in a critical edition of the Suites, to include the ones in A minor and E-flat major (cited above) together with the group of French Suites—to which they belong not only because of their form, but also because of their appearance in the extremely important collections *C* and *D* (see below). I should like to add, in this connection, that I have no point of vantage from which to determine just when Bach selected the six familiar suites out of the entire group of suites written in the manner common to the French Suites. Nevertheless, I am certain that he did make the selection himself. I must also leave unanswered the question why the suites were called "French." Apropos the English Suites—Forkel states that they were composed for an eminent Englishman.

My manuscript source-material for the French Suites is as follows:

    A. The little "Klavierbüchlein" of Anna Magdalena Bach. (Royal Library in Berlin.)

    B. The large "Klavierbüchlein" of Anna Magdalena Bach. (Royal Library in Berlin.)

    C. The Rust-Wagner copy, derived from Friedmann Bach's legacy. (Royal

Library in Berlin.) Documents *A*, *B*, and *C* are actual autographs.

D. Gerber's copies. (Property of Dr. Erich Prieger, Berlin.)

E. A copy of the C minor Suite, spuriously listed in the catalogue as an autograph. (Royal Library in Berlin—P. 274.)

F. A copy of the first E-flat major Suite. (Royal Library in Berlin—P. 289.)

G. A fragment of the G major Suite. (Royal Library in Berlin—P. 212.)

H. A copy of the French Suites originally owned by Kirnberger. (Amalien-library #76.)

J. A complete, more recent copy. (Amalien-library #50.)

K. A copy of the second E-flat major Suite. (Amalien-library #552.)

The following analysis of the relative authoritativeness of these documents will serve to justify my eclectic procedure in reconstructing the text. It will also serve to prove that a positive decision by the editor in certain instances could only be interpreted as an obviously arbitrary action. I sincerely hope that the performer will be interested in studying the different variants from the authentic manuscripts, so that he can make his own logical choice. Our text contains, to be sure, only thoroughly authenticated versions.

A contains the authoritativeness of an early manuscript. One may deviate from it if a later variant bears the stamp of proven authenticity. The little book, dating from 1722, contains twenty-five pages—not all of them in correct sequence. Fragments of the first three French Suites appear in it; the fourth and fifth Suites are complete. The original sequence appears to have been as follows: the third, fourth and fifth Suites were definitely in correct succession, the one in C minor probably preceded them, a fragment of the D minor Suite probably came at the beginning of the little book. I see no reason for assuming a different sequence for the Suites, particularly since the D minor Suite definitely comes first, and the C minor Suite is called the *second*—in *B*. In *A*, several short pieces are written after the G major Suite. They are of little consequence—excepting three Minuets, one belonging to the C minor Suite, another in B minor subsequently added to the Suite in the same key, and one in G major that was probably intended as a supplement to the G major Suite.

B dates from the year 1725. It contains, in addition to some compositions which we do not have to discuss at this point, the complete D minor Suite and the C minor Suite almost up to the end of the Sarabande. The manuscript contains several free variants; moreover, it is written in a very cursory manner. I counted over thirty careless errors in script.

C is an autograph which was passed on from Friedmann Bach to F. W. Rust, then to Dr. W. Rust. In 1844 the firm of Peters received it for the purpose of revising the text. It was then completely lost sight of for over twenty years until it was restored to its owner by Dr. Abraham. Later it was secured by Prof. Wagner in Marburg, who in turn passed it on to the Royal Library in Berlin. The contents of *C* include the Suites in D minor, C minor, B minor, A minor, the second E-flat major Suite, and finally the fourth of the French Suites—i.e., the first Suite in E-flat major. The works were written consecutively; only the second Allemande of the second E-flat Suite was pasted in later, and the Minuet of the first E-flat Suite is of earlier date. One's doubts are awakened by the numerous corrections, some of them made by erasure. The last lines of the Allemande and Courante from the C minor Suite actually appear on strips of paper that were pasted in subsequently. The extent to which these facts affect the authenticity of *C* may be determined by a comparison with *D*.

The *D* collection of manuscripts is of decisive significance in considering all important critical problems. Heinrich Nicolaus Gerber made these copies during the period of his study with Bach. Before me lie the copies of the French Suites (including the supplement), four English Suites, the Inventions and Symphonies, the beginning of the Well-Tempered Clavichord and several other items.

According to the testimony of his son, the lexicographer, Gerber went to Leipzig in May 1724 and became a pupil of Bach half a year later. After two years of study he returned to his home. During the period of his work with Bach he studied the Inventions, many of the Suites, the Well-Tempered Clavichord, finally—thorough-bass. The manuscripts in my possession appear approximately in the above sequence; they belong, in all probability, to the year 1725.

The following succession of the French Suites in Gerber seems to me to be more or less haphazard: 1) D minor, 2) A minor, 3) the second E-flat major Suite, 4) B minor, 5) C minor, 6) the first E-flat major Suite, 7) missing, 8) G major. The title is merely: "Suite pour le Clavecin." It is uncertain just which Suite was intended as #7. It may, perhaps, have been the one in E minor.

Of the English Suites, the Gerber manuscripts contain the ones in A major, G minor, E minor and D minor. The particular value of these copies lies not only in the care and fidelity of the execution of the manuscripts, but also in the fact that they were made during the time of Gerber's actual work with Bach—for purposes of study.

E is a good old manuscript of the C minor Suite. Many of the variants are similar to *B*. It is not particularly authoritative.

F is a copy of the first E-flat Suite in very peculiar form. It contains a Prelude, Allemande, Courante, Sarabande, Gavotte, then another untraditional Gavotte of doubtful quality, finally an Aria. There is no Gigue. This manuscript is interesting in that it takes into consideration some of the doubtful corrections in *C*. But the whole form of the Suite is highly questionable.

In *G*, the Louré of the Fifth Suite is called a Bourée! The Allemande and Gigue are reversed, and written in a handwriting different from the rest of the manuscript. The authoritativeness of *G* is questionable.

H is a manuscript containing all six of the familiar French Suites. It is a good copy; but it is of importance only where the autographs are inadequate. The same can be said of the *J* manuscript. However, both *H* and *J* must be seriously considered in connection with any publication of the E major Suite.

K is a carefully prepared copy of the little E-flat major Suite.

The first five French Suites were composed in 1722, the one in D minor may have been written even earlier. They were probably composed in the same succession as the sequence in which they have traditionally appeared in print. The autographs contain no preludes. In *D*, the E major Suite contains a Prelude; in *F*, the first E-flat major Suite; in Peters, the A minor and E minor Suites—the latter also in *D*. The Minuets in the C minor and B minor Suites were written later.

Insofar as the English Suites are concerned, the province of criticism becomes a much easier field to traverse; for it is much simpler to trace the genesis of these works. The title, "English Suite," is an unimportant nickname. Forkel's explanation that these Suites were ordered by an eminent Englishman is supported by *C*; but the inscription appearing in this manuscript—"fait pour les Anglais" was inscribed on the title-page in a strange handwriting. The true title should be: "Suite avec prélude," i.e., "Suite with a Prelude."

I have utilized the following manuscripts:

A. This is the autograph proper, belonging to Mr. Hauser in Karlsruhe. Spitta was not acquainted with this source. The ending of the first Suite appears in a strange handwriting.

B. The Gerber copies of the Suites in A major, G minor, E minor and D minor. (Compare our discussion of the Gerber copies under *D* of the French Suites.)

C. A manuscript in the possession of Mrs. Mendelssohn in Berlin. It is complete up to the F major Suite. The latter contains the signature: Jean Chrétien Bach. There is no proof that it was really finished by the latter. However, the whole manuscript gains in importance because it had been the property of Johann Christian Bach.

D. A good, complete earlier copy—also belonging to Mrs. Mendelssohn.

E. No. 489 in the Amalien-library. Good and complete.

F. No. 50 in the Amalien-library. Somewhat later than *E*; equally complete and dependable.

G. No. 291 of the Royal Library in Berlin. This is a complete copy.

Fragments of the Suite collections appear in the following:

H. No. 56 in the Amalien-library.

J. No. 212 in the Royal Library in Berlin.

K. No. 218 in the Royal Library in Berlin.

L. This is a collection of five Preludes from the English Suites (the first is omitted). Property of Dr. W. Rust—inherited from the legacy of F. W. Rust.

There are no difficulties in presenting the text. The autograph is a careful "fair copy"; the Gerber manuscripts follow the autograph very literally, even to the inclusion of errors in script. If the authenticity of *A* needed any confirmation, it could certainly be supplied by *B*. I believe it is highly probable that *B* was copied directly from *A*; the proof of this lies in the similarity of many of the errata. It is only in relation to these errata that our sources from *C* to *L* become important. There are very few deviations in the form of the Suites. In *A*, the continuity of the Suites is sustained. If *B* is a direct copy of *A*, then we are justified in believing that all the English Suites (including those not appearing in Gerber) were completed by 1725. One can be just as certain of the continuity of the six Suites as one is of the construction of the individual Suites. In the English Suites we have a collection which Bach himself put together; in the French Suites we assume that his final intention is the familiar traditional selection of six Suites.

As a final note I should like to mention that I have not always taken into consideration the extremely detailed indication of ties and dots in the autographs. The ties appearing in heavier type are traditional.[1] All the ornaments appearing in the text, including the quick appoggiaturas indicated by little apostrophes, are authentic.

Dr. Hans Bischoff
Berlin, 1881

---

[1] There is no differentiation between "heavy" and "thin" ties in this edition.

TABLE OF EMBELLISHMENTS

For the uninitiated performer the following indications will suffice—in reference to this volume.

1) Grace notes, like all other embellishments, enter ON the beat—not before it. Unless indicated otherwise, they should be executed quickly.

2) The trill (*tr* or ⁓) generally begins on the auxiliary note. There is usually an after-beat, unless this is replaced by one or more indicated notes. The after-beat is unnecessary before a descending second. The symbol for the trill with an upbeat is ⁓ or ⁓. The trill starting on the lower note ⁓ and the one starting on the upper note ⁓ usually both end with an after-beat. The following symbols may also be used to indicate the same: ⁓ and ⁓. The short trill ⁓ is usually tied to the upper second preceding. Its symbol frequently takes the place of ⁓ and *tr*.

3) The mordent ⁓ or ⁓ often takes the tone a minor second lower as the auxiliary note, although the neighboring note is sometimes a major second lower.

4) The turn ∞ placed over a note is executed ⁓, placed between two notes it is played ⁓. In dotted rhythm, the turn proper ends on the dot ⁓.

5) The slurred note ⁓ is played ⁓.

6) Other embellishments are explained in the annotations.

Dr. Hans Bischoff

Six English Suites
Suite No. 1 in A Major

Johann Sebastian Bach (1685–1750)
BWV 806

1) G-natural in *F*.
2) A-sharp in *D* and *F*.

1) In the manuscripts the tying of the notes is frequently inconsistent.

1) The lower A played by the right hand appears in *C*.
2) The sharp before the D in the printed editions is not authenticated by the manuscripts. However, the parallel passage at the end of the piece, in the measure before the last, does have a G-sharp.

NB. The oblique lines in the middle of the intervals are probably meant to indicate abbreviated mordents, i.e. acciaccaturas.

Their execution would be as follows: [musical example]. The extra tone is played simultaneously with the third and then immediately released. An arpeggio sign may have been intended before the oblique line. There are many examples in Bach of the

"arpeggio with an acciaccatura": [musical example]. The same is found in Ph. E. Bach, written as follows: [musical example].

Compare the Sarabande of this Suite. The non-arpeggiated acciaccatura sounds too harsh in the above passage. I advise the execution indicated at ⊕. Others suggest ordinary broken thirds.

1) In *E* and *G* one finds the following distorted version:
2) In *B* there also appear little apostrophes above the E and the F-sharp, probably meant to indicate appoggiaturas.

DOUBLE I

1) In *B* both Doubles contain the B, analogously to the theme. The other manuscripts frequently contain a D instead of the B.

1) C instead of C-sharp, in *D* and *F*.

DOUBLE II

1) in *E* and *G*.

2) See note 1 to the first double.

3) The natural sign is missing in *B*.

1) G-sharp instead of G, in *B*.

2) in *E* and *G*.

1) Here and elsewhere the rhythm in *D* and *F* appears as follows:
2) According to *D* and *F* the first appoggiatura is a D instead of C-sharp.
3) The appoggiatura A appears in *B*; others have an F-sharp.

NB. 1. 2. These are examples of the "arpeggio with an acciaccatura." The execution is

or perhaps . The broken notes in the right hand are to be played quickly; all are sustained—excepting the inharmonic tone.

1) The F-sharp is an eighth-note in *C, D, E* and *F*.
2) Our text is according to *B, C* and *D*. Elsewhere one finds:
3) The majority of the ties in this movement are authentic, with the exception of a few additions and corrections by the author. The phrasing usually indicated　　　　　　　is not authentic.

1) I must offer the suggestion that Bach may have intended the following execution of the next seven measures: [music example] etc. The notation of the ties seems to have been done very cursorily.

2) The execution is "portamento." The following notation is possible: [music example]

3) In reference to the first two measures and their repetition—compare note 1.

1) F instead of F-sharp in *B*—an error in script.

2) Longer trills are presumably intended here, e.g.,

1) Variant appearing only in F:

2) The indication, "piano," appears in the manuscripts. Various editions contain a D-sharp in this measure, analogously to the similar passage appearing near the end of the movement; however, the manuscripts do not contain the sharp sign.

1) Our text appears in *A* and *B*; others contain [music example] or [music example]
2) G-sharp instead of G in *E* and *G*.

Suite No. 2 in A Minor

BWV 807

PRÉLUDE

1) The grace-notes always appearing with this theme are to be found in *A*, where they are indicated by apostrophes. The Bach-Gesellschaft edition erroneously interprets these apostrophes as ties.

ALLEMANDE
Allegretto (♩ = 92)

1) B instead of A in *A*, through an error in script. This mistake reappears in the Bach-Gesellschaft edition.

1) The sharp sign is missing in *E* and *G*.
2) Several manuscripts contain a tie between the two A's in the soprano.

1) [music example] in *E* and *G*.

2) In several of the manuscripts the tie in the soprano is omitted. Similarly in the final measure of the piece.

NB. Many of the eighth-note groups contain ties in the manuscripts.

1) Several manuscripts contain a sustaining tie between these two notes.
2) In *A* the turn appears over the F.
3) See note 2, page 38.
4) This is tied in *E* and *G*.

Les agréments de la même Sarabande [4]

1) The G is missing in *A*.
2) This is tied in *E* and *G*.
3) This mordent seems questionable to me. However, it appears in *A*; it is missing in *C* and *D*.
4) The "Agréments" movement is missing in *F*. Most of the sources contain only the upper voice; in *C*, the exact bass of the Sarabande is added to the upper voice of the "Agréments." The fragments of the middle voice printed on the extra staff in small type are derived from the *D* manuscript. Our fingerings assume that the middle voice is played.
5) C instead of B—an error in script in *A*. This error has been widely reprinted; however, it has been duly corrected in the Bach-Gesellschaft edition.

BOURRÉE I (alternativement)
Allegro vivace ($\quarter = 100$)

1) This ornament is according to *A*. Elsewhere one finds:

1) The indication regarding the "repeat" appearing below the 2nd ending is missing in *D* and *F*.

Suite No. 3 in G Minor

1) In most of the manuscripts as well as in the Autograph, the natural before the E is missing in the opening section; but it does appear at the beginning of the recapitulation.

2) Our text is the one which is most authentic. However, the *E* and *K* version, has been used in most of the printed editions; and it has the advantage of closer conformity with other parallel passages.

3) In *A* and *B* one finds the obvious error in script in place of

1) The natural sign before the E is missing in *A*, *B* and *G*.

2) In *A* and *B*:

1) It is singular that the E-flat is missing in both chords in *A, B, C, D* and *G*.

1) In D and F:

1) The D is missing in *A* and *B*.

2) E instead of E-flat—an error in script in *A* and *B*.

3) In *C* the measure following was originally omitted.
   Through subsequent correction the two measures took the following form:

1) According to D and F the middle voice is: [music example]. At + there is a C instead of the D, in both A and B—through an error in script.

1) Several fingerings appear in the following passage in *A* and *B*.

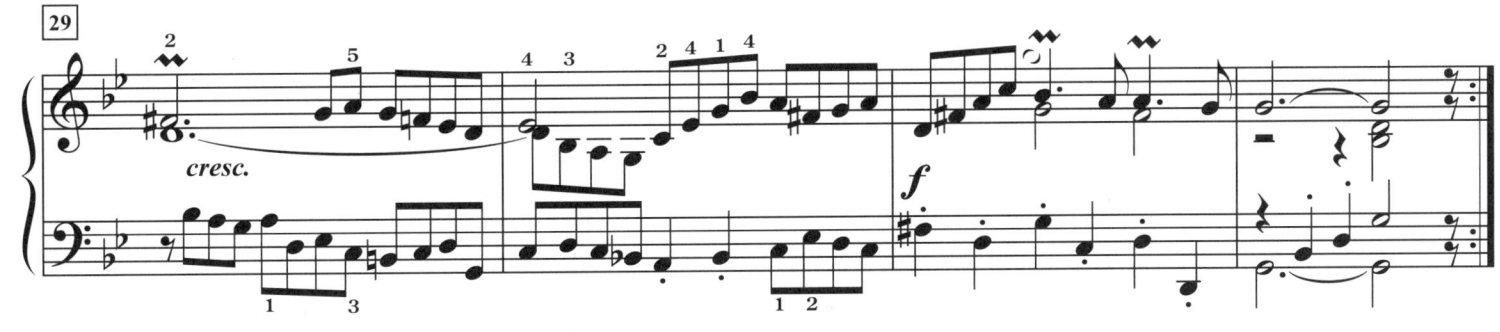

1) Before the written grace-notes there were still others indicated by apostrophes; their execution would approximately be as follows:

1) This "Agréments" movement appears in *A* and *B*.

2) According to *B*:

NB. 1   NB. 2

3) This altogether extraordinary C-natural appears in *A* and *B*. Perhaps a D was intended. Compare the analogous passage in the simple Sarabande.

4) Here, too, there are apostrophes before the grace-notes. Compare to note 1 to the Sarabande.

5) The note values are inexact in the manuscripts.

1) F instead of D, an error in script in *B*.

GAVOTTE II (ou la Musette)

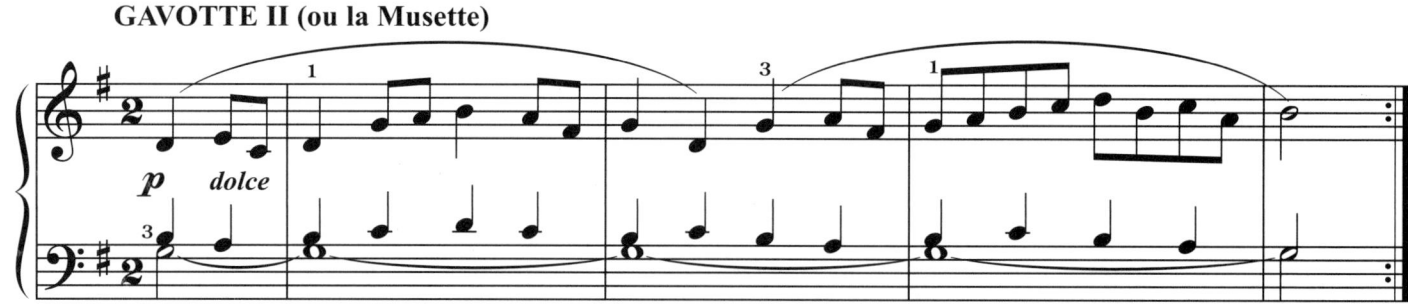

Das zweite Mal noch schwächer

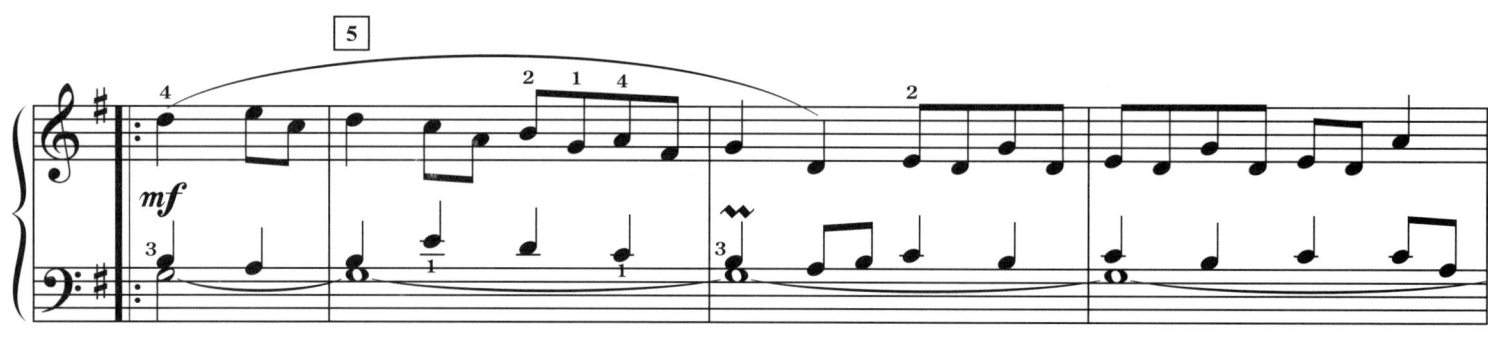

1) In *A* and *B*: ♪

2) ♪ *sic!* in *C*. At + one finds F-sharp instead of G also in *E* and *G*.

1) in *D* and *F*.

1) In *D* and *F* these two notes are: F-sharp, E-natural.

Suite No. 4 in F Major

PRÉLUDE
Allegro (♩ = 108)

BWV 809

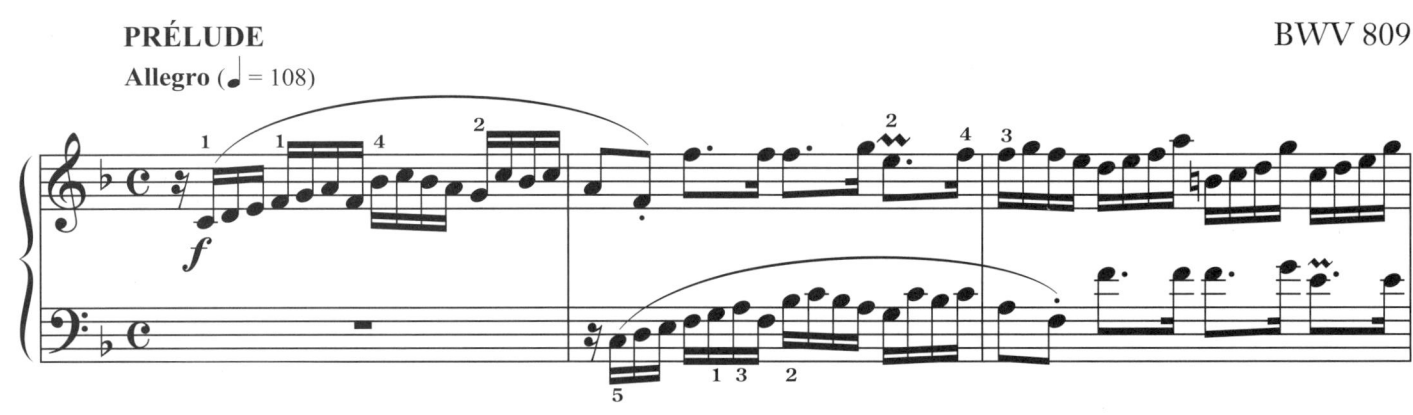

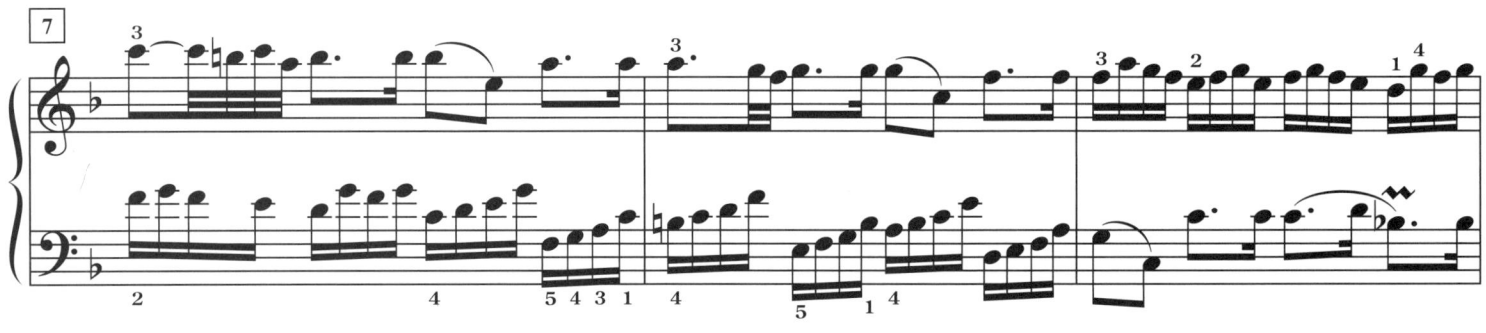
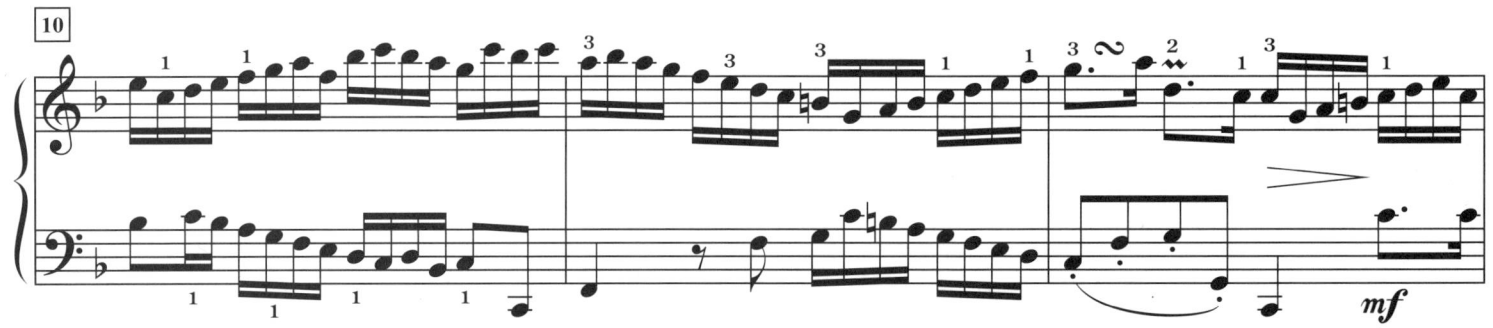

1) G instead of B-flat—an error in script in *A*.

2) In *D* and *F*:

3) in *D* and *F*.

4) in *E*; in *G*.

1) in *D* and *F*.

1) In D and F:

1) One occasionally finds the following error in script:

1) In *D* the natural sign is missing; in *F* there is a flat sign before the E.
2) In *A* the B-flat is replaced by a D. Our text is based on *D* and *F*. *E* is as follows:
3) Our text is based on *D*, *E*, *F*, *G* and *L*. In *A* there is an E, but without the natural sign.

1) ♪♪♪ in *D* and *F*.

2) The reading in *D* and *F* is: ♩

1) It is extraordinary that this natural sign is missing in all the manuscripts.

1) It is quite possible that a natural sign before the B was omitted.

COURANTE
Allegro (𝅗𝅥 = 80)

1) In E: [music example] ; moreover, the natural sign is missing at +.

1) Many additional ornaments appear in *E* and *G*.

2) C instead of D, according to *D* and *F*.

3) According to *E* and *G*: . Our text is authentic throughout; the natural sign before the A on the third beat originates with the editor.

1) Here and in few other places in this Gigue, there appear barely recognizable errors in script in *A*; these are scarcely worth noting.

NB. It is left to the imagination of the performer whether or not to include the mordent at this point.

1) an error in script in *A*.

Suite No. 5 in E Minor

BWV 810

PRÉLUDE
Allegro (♩. = 80)

1) ; an error in script in *A* and *B*.

1) B instead of E, an error in script in *A* and *B*.

1) B instead of C-sharp, in *E* and *G*.

1) This F-sharp is absolutely authentic, even though the construction is not in agreement with analogous sequences.
2) The sharp before the C is missing in most of the manuscripts.
NB. In the editor's opinion, the trills printed in smaller type should be played.

NB. A long trill.

1) In *A* the "da capo" indication appears in the left hand one measure too soon. (The Preludes are generally written out only up to the recapitulation of the opening section.) In *B* one finds the following transition:

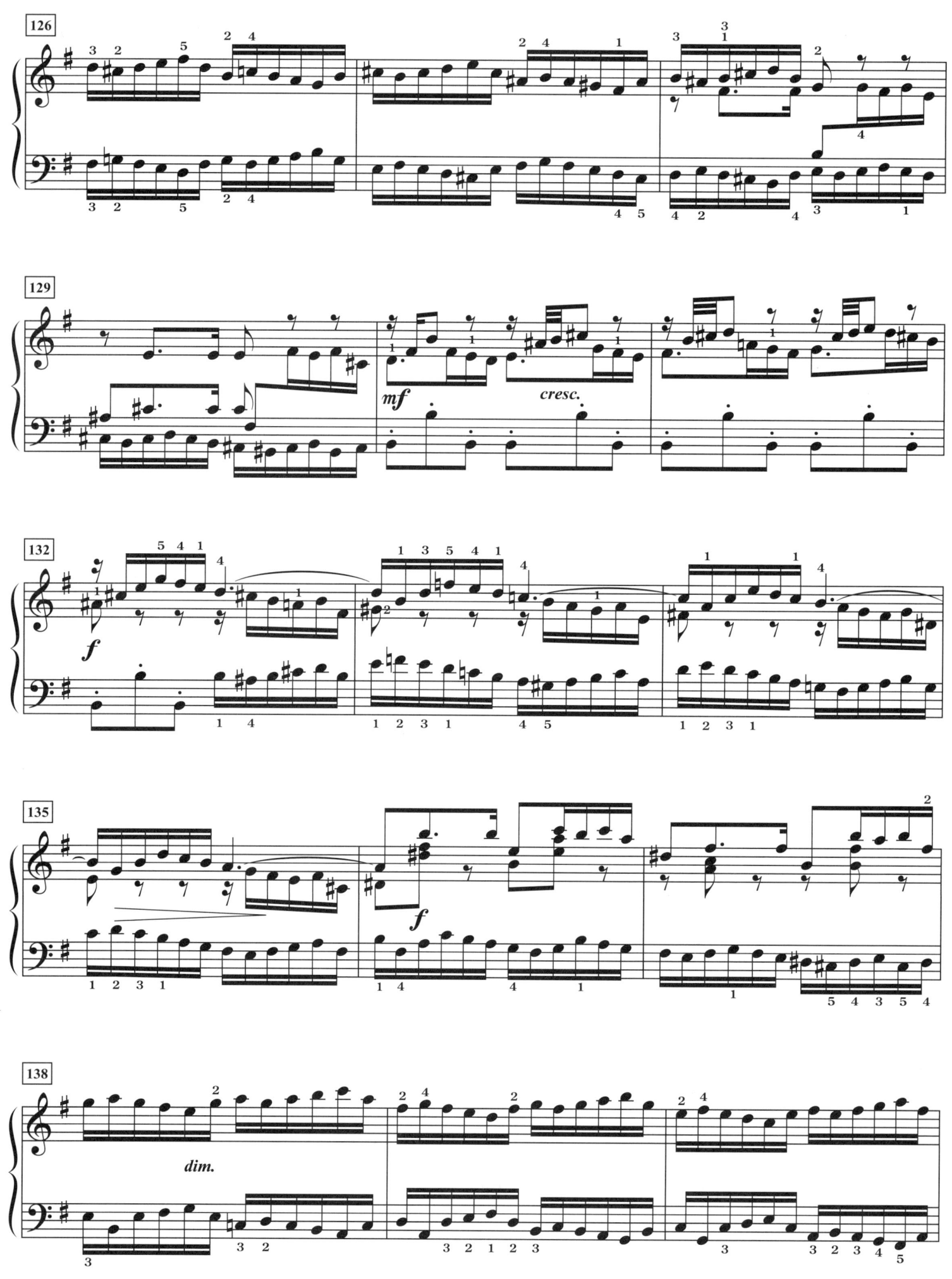

1) An error in script in *A* and *B*:

1) According to *C*: E instead of D. Compare the previous measure.

COURANTE
Allegro (♩ = 160)

1) C instead of D—in F.

1) The sharp is missing in *A, B* and *G*.
2) There are apostrophes before the grace-notes in *A, B* and *E*.

1) Here and in the next measure both hands contain ♪♪ according to *E* and *G*.
2) According to *A, B, D* and *G*, there are no sharps before the G and A.

PASSEPIED II

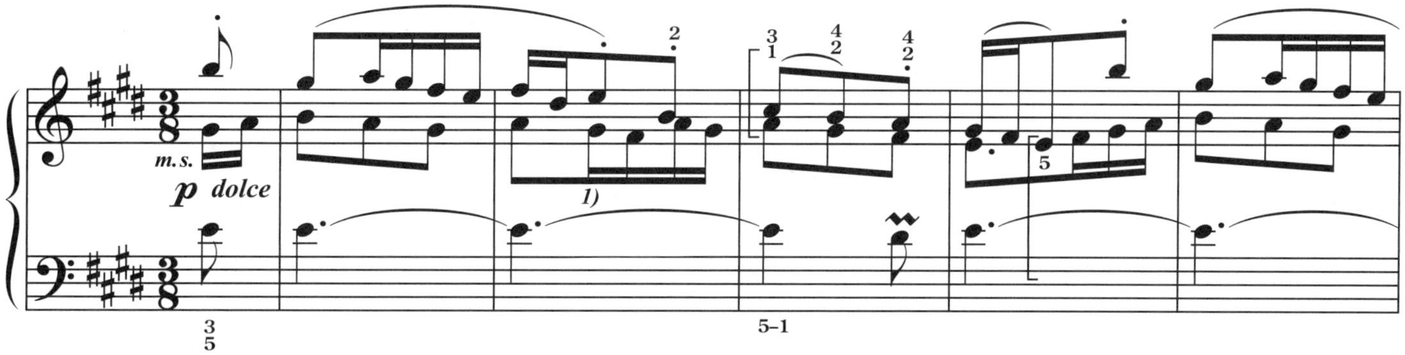

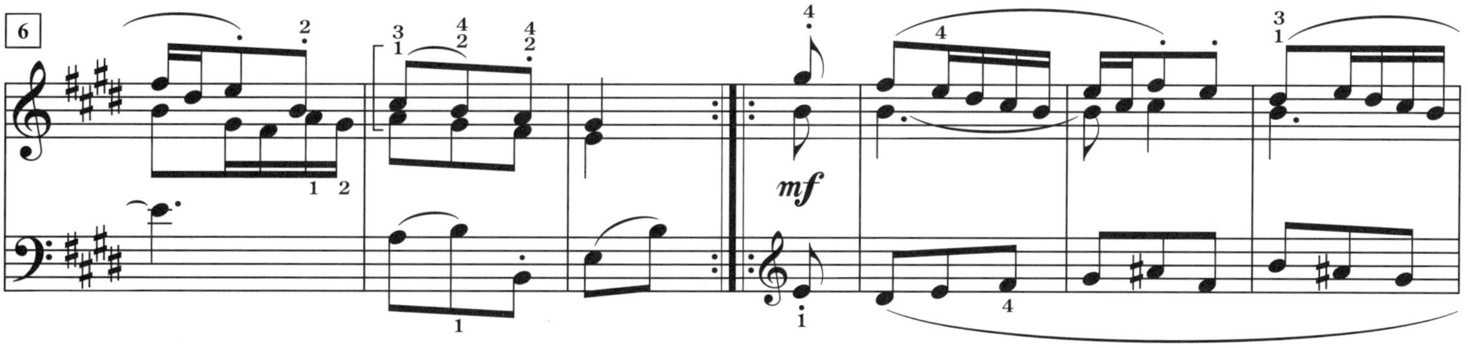

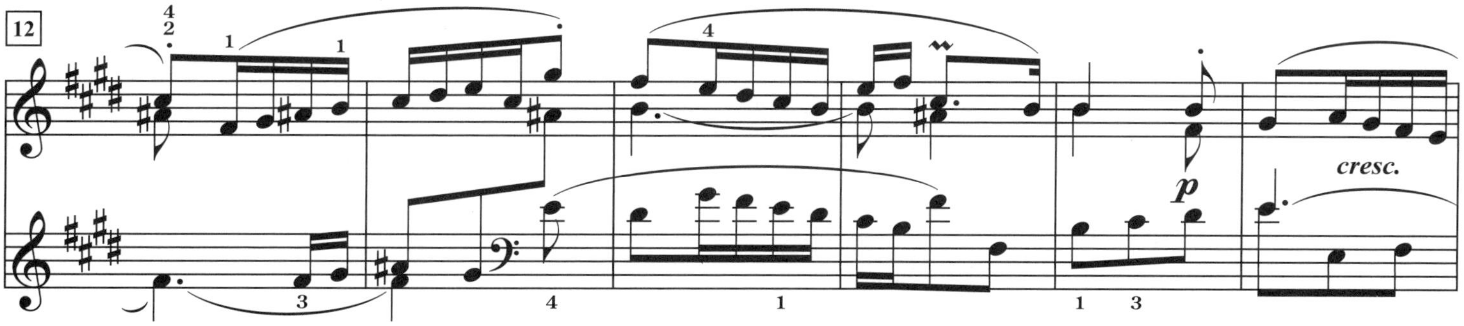

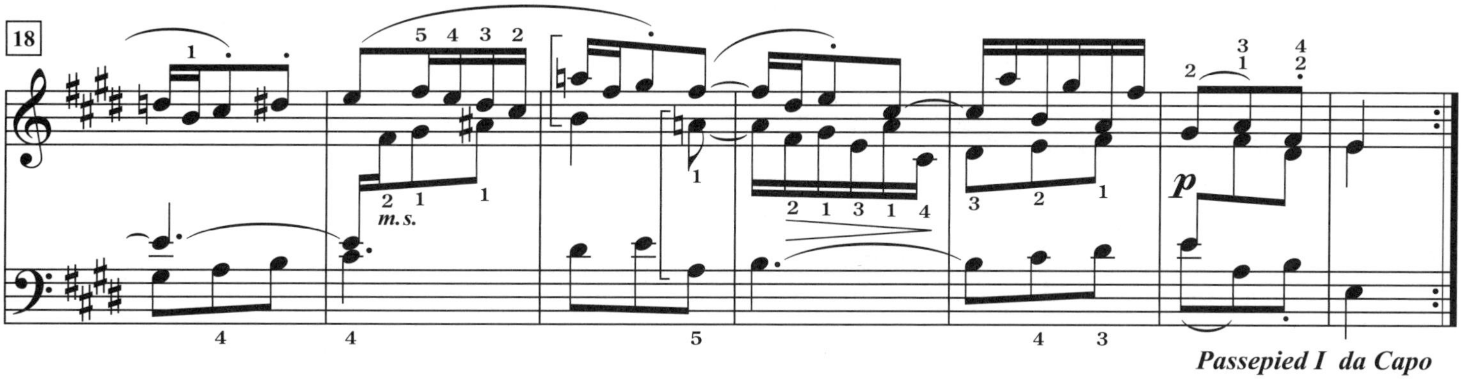

Passepied I da Capo

1) The middle voice according to *E* and *G*: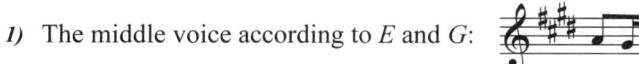

1) The sharp is missing in *D* and *F*.
2) C-sharp, according to *D* and *F*.
3) The sharp before the A is missing in *B*. It is questionable in *A*.
4) [music example] in *C*.
5) The sharp is missing in *C, E, G* and *J*.

1) According to C, E and G:

Suite No. 6 in D Minor

PRÉLUDE

Moderato (♩. = 66)

BWV 811

1) Some of the ties are inexact in the sources.

1) in *A* and *B*.

1) One finds the following misprint in the Bach-Gesellschaft edition and elsewhere:

2) B-natural instead of B-flat, according to *E, G* and *K*.

1) C instead of A, an error in script in *A* and *B*.
NB. The quarter-note stems have been added by the editor.

1) According to *A* and *B*: F instead of E.
2) According to *C* and *D*: C instead of B-flat.
3) G-sharp in *D, F* and *K*.

1) an error in script in *A* and *B*.

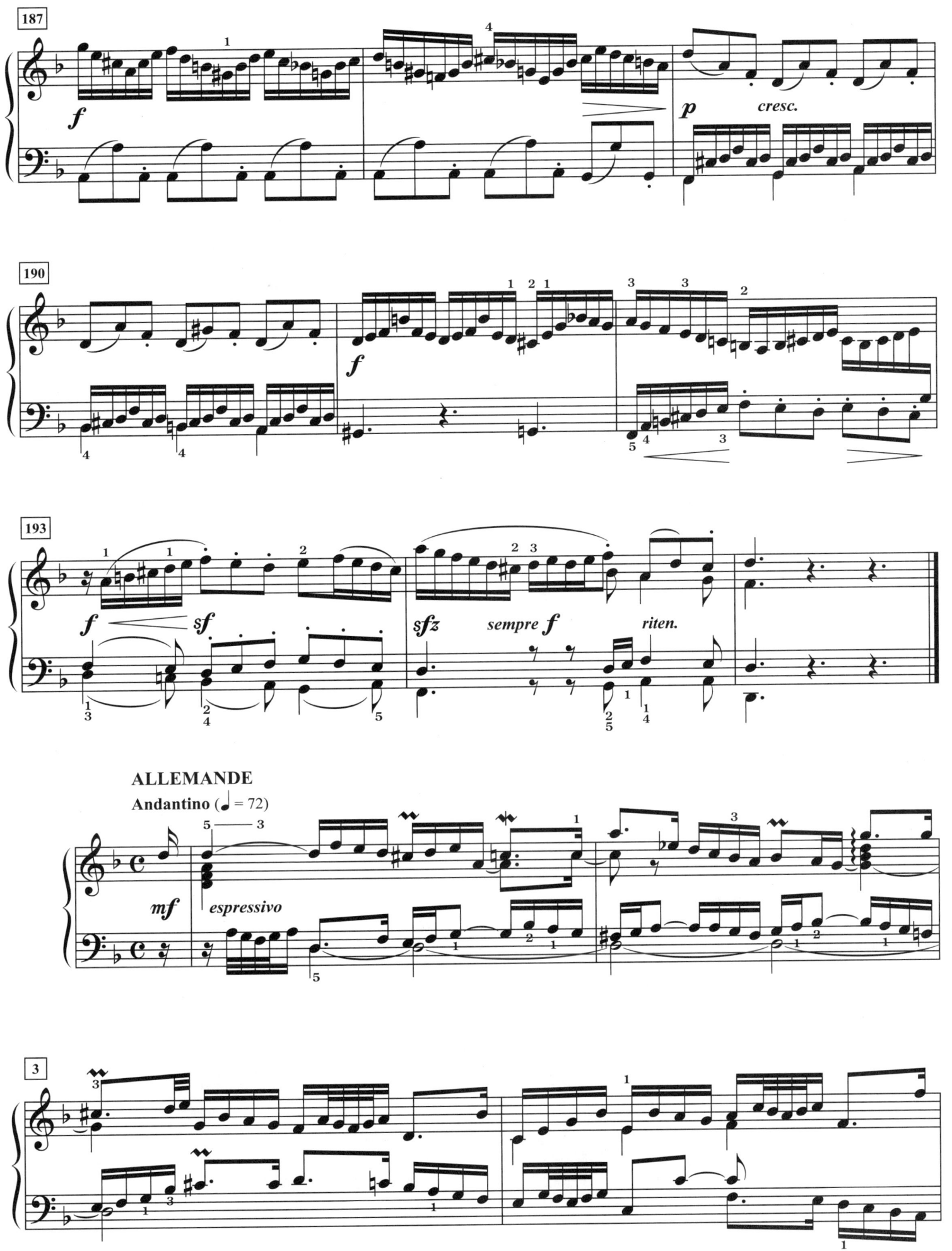

1) The natural sign is missing in *A* and *B*.

1) In *B*, quarter-notes in place of ♩. ♪.
2) A-flat instead of A, in *D* and *F*.
3) D instead of E, an error in script in *A* and *B*.
4) [bass figure] in *C*.

1) The flat before the A is missing in many of the manuscripts.

SARABANDE
Sostenuto (♩ = 63)

Il basso marcato

1) B instead of D, in *E, G* and *K*.

1) According to *C, D* and *F*:
2) According to *A* and *B, E*-sharp!
3) None of the manuscripts contain a C-sharp.

1) The ornaments in small type appearing in conjunction with the rhythm ♩. ♫ must be played. They appear in *D* and *F*. They are always long trills.

126

NB. The fingering is:

1) According to *A, B, D* and *F*:
2) E instead of D, in *D* and *F*.

Gavotte I da Capo

1) E instead of F-sharp, in *E, G* and *K*.

1) The natural sign is missing in *A* and *B*.

1) There is a natural sign in *E, G* and *K*.
2) The sharp is missing in *A* and *B*.